P9-DCP-569

Months of the Year

June

by Mari Kesselring
Illustrated by Roberta Collier-Morales

Content Consultant:
Susan Kesselring, MA
Literacy Educator and Preschool Director

visit us at www.abdopublishing.com

Published by Magic Wagon, a division of the ABDO Group, 8000 West 78th Street, Edina, Minnesota 55439.

Printed in the United States.

Text by Mari Kesselring
Illustrations by Roberta Collier-Morales
Edited by Patricia Stockland
Interior layout and design by Emily Love
Cover design by Emily Love

Library of Congress Cataloging-in-Publication Data

Kesselring, Mari.
June / by Mari Kesselring ; illustrated by Roberta Collier-Morales ; content consultant, Susan Kesselring.
p. cm. — (Months of the year)
ISBN 978-1-60270-633-0
1. June (Month)—Juvenile literature. 2. Calendar—Juvenile literature. I. Collier-Morales, Roberta, ill. II. Kesselring, Susan. III. Title.
CE13.K475 2010
398'.33—dc22

2008050707

This question will
put you in a fix.
Do you know the name
of month number six?

Yes! It's June!
Thirty days of fun.
Six more months
until the year is done.

October
September
November
August
JULY
June
JUNE
May

June was named after
a queen called Juno.
She was a goddess
of married women long ago.

June is when
the school year ends.
Get ready to play
outside with your friends!

List all the fun things to do during June.

Put some flowers in pots. Hear a bird sing a tune!

·skateboard
·swim
·long walks
·camp
Picnics
Cook-outs
·Go hiking
·fishing
plant a garden
go to movie
Play dates
walk the dog
go to the park

June is Dairy Month. Have some milk treats.
Try cheese or yogurt or ice cream sweets!

Did you know Flag Day
is on day 14?
Hang up a flag
so it can be seen.

June 18 is Picnic Day.
Pack a good lunch.
Watch out for the ants.
They might like to munch!

Father's Day might
make you glad.
The third Sunday in June
is just for Dad!

The first day of summer is also in June.
Enjoy a campfire. Gaze up at the moon.

This fun summer month
is over so soon.
But July is the great month
that comes after June!

JULY

Make Your Own American Flag

Celebrate Flag Day by making your own flag. Have an adult help you cut out a paper rectangle. Draw a big blue square in the top left corner. Draw the red stripes. Put star stickers in the blue rectangle. Roll up a piece of newspaper tightly to make a pole for the flag. When you are done drawing the flag, tape it to the newspaper pole. Now you have a flag for Flag Day!

Ice Cream!

Make an ice cream sundae for Dairy Month. Don't forget hot fudge and a lot of cherries!

Words to Know

dairy—milk and food that is made from milk.
gaze—to look at something.
July—the seventh month of the year. It comes after June.
picnic—a meal that you eat outside.

Web Sites

To learn more about June, visit ABDO Group online at **www.abdopublishing.com**. Web sites about June are featured on our Book Links page. These links are routinely monitored and updated to provide the most current information available.